PORTABLE

COLOUR ME

STRESS-FREE

Quarto is the authority on a wide range of topics.

Quarto educates, entertains and enriches the lives of our readers—enthusiasts and lovers of hands-on living.

www.quartoknows.com

First published in the United States of America in 2016 by Race Point Publishing, a member of Quarto Publishing Group USA Inc.
142 West 36th Street, 4th Floor
New York, New York 10018
www.quartoknows.com

10 9 8 7 6 5 4 3 2 1

ISBN 978-1-63106-268-1

Editorial Director: Jeannine Dillon
Managing Editor: Erin Canning
Project Editor: Jason Chappell
Cover Design: Jacqui Caulton
Interior Design: Rosamund Saunders

Printed in China

This book provides general information on various widely known and widely accepted images that tend to evoke feelings of calm and/or reduced stress or anxiety in individuals. However, it should not be relied upon as recommending or promoting any specific diagnosis or method of treatment for a particular condition, and it is not intended as a substitute for medical advice or for direct diagnosis and treatment of a medical condition by a qualified physician. Readers who have questions about a particular condition, possible treatments for that condition, or possible reactions from the condition or its treatment should consult a physician or other qualified health care professional.

PORTABLE
COLOUR ME
STRESS-
FREE

70 Colouring Templates
to Unplug and Unwind

Lacy Mucklow, MA, ATR-BC, LPAT, LCPAT

Illustrated by Angela Porter

Race Point
PUBLISHING

CONTENTS

INTRODUCTION

Why create a colouring book for adults? As children, many of us enjoyed colouring our favorite characters or scenes in books with our trusty pack of crayons. But as we got older, added responsibilities came along that pushed aside things we used to do for sheer enjoyment.

One of the great things about colouring is that it is highly successful for everyone—even if you lack artistic instruction or experience—and it can be as nuanced or generalised as the colourer wishes. Having guidelines eases performance anxiety, and being able to add our own colours helps make the experience more personal. The act of colouring can also be meditative in and of itself, bringing about stress relief just through the simple act of picking up a coloured pencil or crayon and focusing creativity and thoughts on a single colouring exercise.

Despite what you may have learned about art and colour in your lifetime, there is no right or wrong way to use this book; you have the freedom to colour it in however you wish in whatever way works best for you. Conceptually, in "Portable Colour Me Stress-Free," the chapters are divided into seven of the most common stressors experienced by people worldwide: disorganization and chaos, relationships of all kinds, financial difficulties, employment, health concerns, time management, and traveling and commuting. We have named the stressors here because sometimes even being able to identify the source of your stress can help to start alleviating it. The images included in this book to colour have been chosen specifically to serve as positive counters to these stressors. These images—mandalas, geometric designs, fractals, and abstract representations—along with themes or structures can provide a feeling of relief from or empowerment towards the stress. For example, images of symmetry, balance, and stability can help to counter the stress that stems from disorganization and chaos. Themes of connectedness, efficiency, regulation, self-care, growth, strength, well-being, order, positive creativity and outcomes, expansion, new beginnings, problem-solving, love, self-reflection, centering, and clear journeys come through the images to help evoke positive qualities that can manage feelings of anxiety and promote a sense of relaxation from daily and chronic stressors.

We realize that what relieves stress for people can run the gamut even within "universal" categories, so we have included a variety of images within each chapter so at least some of the pieces connect with you personally. The designs are intended for adult sensibility and dexterity rather than for children, and include actual scenes (or variations thereof) of stress-relieving subjects. Many are more abstract in nature so that you may enjoy the intricacy of the patterns themselves, as many of us do. Most importantly, this book is about helping you suspend your mental energies for a short while and hone in on something else that can help promote well-being.

At the end of each chapter, a blank panel has been included so that you can have a chance to think about and draw (and colour) an image that is uniquely stress-relieving to you—this will make the colouring experience even more personal and will hopefully keep you mindful about things and experiences that you find relaxing. You may find that using this book regularly might be particularly helpful for you, such as beginning your morning with a colouring template to help you set a calm and mindful tone for the day or colouring before going to sleep to help your body and mind to wind down from the day. Or you may choose to use it as needed, in response to a particularly long day or after excess exposure to one particular stressor.

This book is intended to help bring you to a more relaxed emotional state as a way to help you self-soothe; however, it is not meant to replace the services of a professional therapist if more direct intervention and personal guidance are needed. We hope that you enjoy this book and that it helps you find a way to colour yourself stress-free!

COLOUR TIP

Cool colours (especially blue, green, and sometimes purple) are considered to have calming qualities, while warmer colours (such as red, oranges, and yellows) have more activating qualities. Bright colours also tend to have more energy, while pastel or tinted colours tend to communicate softer energy. Darker colours or shades usually indicate lower energy. The most important thing to consider when colouring is to determine which pleasant and soothing colours will help you when you need to calm down, and which energetic colours will help you when you want to promote a positive growth or outlook, and then try to incorporate them into your artwork.

Chapter 1

DISORGANISATION

Stressors can impact us even more deeply when the source of the stress is something over which we feel we should have a certain amount of control. Living or working in a disorganised home or workspace can be especially stressful for that reason. Clutter can make you feel unsettled in your home (a place to retreat and relax) or at work (where you are meant to be productive). When it is difficult to locate an item due to clutter, this can subsequently add to feelings of anxiety and simultaneously trigger other stress reactions. One way to combat the stress induced by disorganisation is to focus on something balanced and orderly. The following images include designs that are symmetrical and balanced in their composition, which can help counter the sense of chaos around you. The act of colouring can also help to dissipate the stress and help you gain a sense of control. Engaging in this process may even help re-center and re-energize you to make a positive influence in your physical environment. A blank panel is included at the end of the chapter to encourage you to draw and colour an image that you especially find balancing and centering.

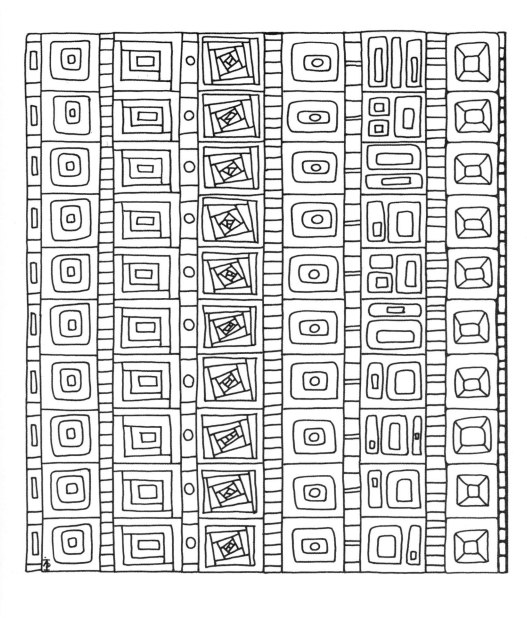

Chapter 2

RELATIONSHIPS

There is no doubt that other people—familiar or strange—can be a major life stressor. And though a person's poor behaviors can be purposeful, they can also happen unintentionally. Dealing with difficult family members, people who have maladaptive behaviors, large crowds, or those with whom we may have tense moments or conflicts can bring on extraordinarily high levels of stress. On the flip side, sometimes even good things that happen in relation to other people (such as a new marriage or birth of a child) can also induce some anxiety. The following soothing designs can help you meditate and de-stress from the complications that can result from interpersonal interactions. Spirals, labyrinths, and upward-facing triangles are just a few symbolic examples of new journeys and fresh beginnings. A blank panel is included at the end of the chapter to encourage you to draw and colour an image that you find particularly stress-relieving.

Chapter 3

FINANCES

One of the perpetual stressors in the history of mankind is finances, particularly personal finances and having enough provisions to meet your family's needs. Whether our situations are temporarily or more permanently affected with a tight budget, living from paycheck to paycheck, trying to stay within financial restrictions, or having difficulty earning a living due to a life circumstance (such as illness, downsizing, caregiving, etc.) can produce stress over the short- or long-term. There can be other kinds of financial stress within our culture besides basic survival: pressure to keep up with trends and the expected "standard of living," which could include the latest technology or fashion. Even more noble pursuits such as the weight of student loans in order to pursue an education can be stressful. The following images are geometric in nature and imbue a sense of stability, productivity, growth, expansion, and new beginnings as a way to help relieve worry associated with finances. A blank panel is included at the end of the chapter to encourage you to draw and colour an image that you may find particularly helpful to de-stress financially.

Chapter 4

WORK

Without question, one of life's biggest daily stressors is from our place of employment. No matter whether you are pursuing a chosen career or simply working at a job that helps make ends meet, there are many on-the-job factors that can add stress to one's life. Whether it's one of the more negative stressors—such as dealing with difficult supervisors, co-workers, or customers; meeting deadlines; handling bureaucracy; fending off burnout or compassion fatigue; managing a high workload; or not meeting expectations—or generally positive stressors—such as gaining added responsibilities due to a promotion; adding value to other people's lives as a result of the work that you do; or tackling rewarding challenges—there are a number of variables that can add pressure to our daily lives. The following images are meant to provide a sense of order and stability through symmetry, while allowing for some creativity, to help you lower the strain you may be experiencing at work. A blank panel is included at the end of the chapter to encourage you to draw and colour an image that you personally find centering.

Chapter 5

HEALTH

Health concerns are common stressors among adults, especially as we get older. Sometimes there are anxieties about maintaining a healthy lifestyle, such as getting enough exercise, eating well, or keeping an ideal weight, especially amidst a busy schedule. In addition, there are also increasing medical issues, as well as medical costs, that tend to come with aging. Even if your health is good, sometimes the concern can come from a family member or friend who may be ill, and stress can come from either being a caregiver for that person or from obstacles that prevent you from helping a loved one. Managing the stress associated with health is paramount to maintaining your health, since stress can take a toll mentally and emotionally, and not just physically. The following images will help you focus on supporting health concerns through abstract and fractal images that represent and promote growth, strength, and well-being. A blank panel is included at the end of the chapter to encourage you to draw and colour a personal design that you may find helpful in maintaining your well-being.

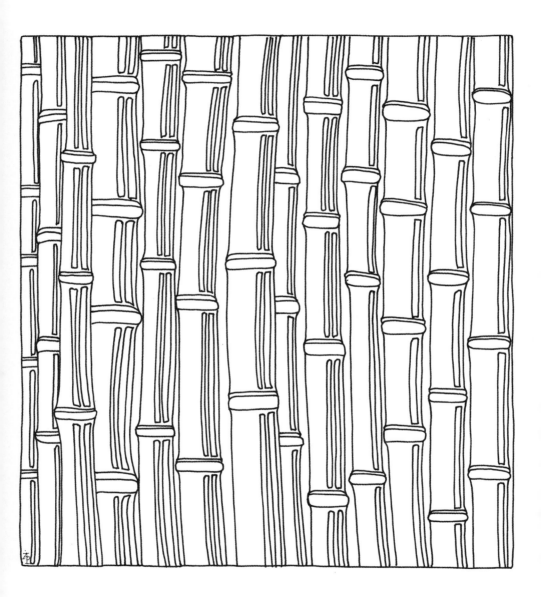

Chapter 6

TIME

Time is one of the most precious commodities in our human existence, and managing it can induce great amounts of stress. It often seems as though we do not have enough time to accomplish all that needs to be done—not only in a day, but also in a lifetime—and there is added pressure when we are running late, feel rushed, or have too many commitments that vie for our attention. Many of us are, unfortunately, participating in today's "too busy" culture, and our lives are comprised of careers, family, errands, daily upkeep, hobbies, and social activities. As naturally linear beings, we have to prioritize and then determine what things need to come first, which not only include fulfilling our responsibilities, but also caring for ourselves. By incorporating self-care, we purposely make time to decompress and recharge so that we can more effectively manage ourselves when we are under pressure. The images in this chapter focus on time management and evoke a sense of self-care, balance, efficiency, and regulation. A blank panel is included at the end of the chapter to encourage you to draw and colour an image that helps you feel balanced.

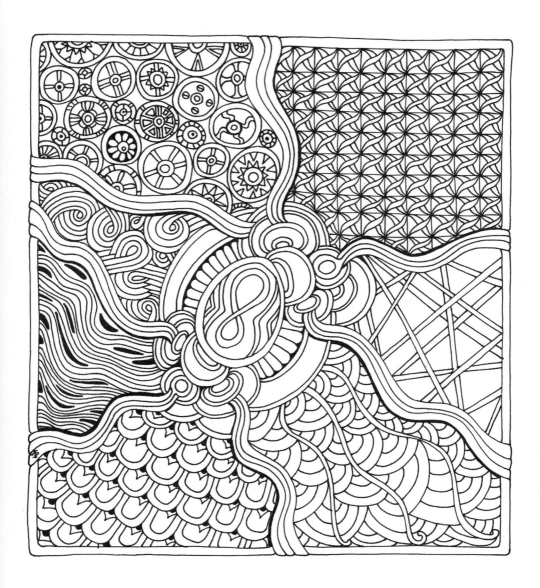

Chapter 7

TRAVEL AND COMMUTING

Whether you are flying internationally or just commuting to work, travel can put an extreme amount of stress on people. Certain aspects of travel—such as sitting in traffic, going through security lines, dealing with inconsiderate people, coordinating public transportation, finding an unfamiliar location, or managing the time it takes to get from Point A to Point B—can cause added stress and affect one's day and interaction with others. The energy it takes to travel—physically, mentally, and even emotionally—can be draining, and we need some restoration time to unwind and recharge so that we can manage the responsibilities that are at our actual destination. The following images are intended to help you visualize clear pathways and positive outcomes. The fractal-style images will help neutralize some of the stress associated with the mechanics of traveling, and a selection of meditative images will help to balance the journey. A blank panel is included at the end of the chapter to encourage you to draw and colour an image that is helpful to your specific travel stressor(s).